I0841634

TAKING CARE OF YOUR EMOTIONS & MIND

IMPORTANT GUIDE FOR YOUR MENTAL HEALTH AND WELLBEING.

2

Contents

3

4

FORWARD

What qualities most accurately characterize mental health?

All facets of our physical, psychological, and mental wellbeing are considered to be part of our mental health. It has an impact on our attitudes, emotions, and behavior. It also has an impact on how we handle stress, interact with people, and make sensible decisions. From youth until maturity, everyone needs to maintain healthy mental health.

What are instances of mental health?

Many mental health issues

- Anger.
- Explains what anger is and offers suggestions about how to manage it in a productive and healthy manner.
- Bipolar disorder,
- body dimorphic disorder (BDD),
- borderline personality disorder (BPD), anxiety and panic attacks, depression,
- Body dimorphic disorder (BDD), and so on.
- Dissociation and disorders associated with it.
- Eating issues.

Typical Myths about Mental Illness

- "Young people and children don't experience mental health issues," is a common myth.

- A mental health issue that seriously impairs a person's capacity to function at home, at school, or in their community is thought to affect more than six million young people in America.

- Myth: "Those who require mental health treatment should be segregated in institutions."

- Fact: Thanks to a range of support services, treatments, and/or drugs, the majority of individuals today can live fulfilling lives in their communities.

- The idea that someone who has had mental illness can never be normal.

- Myth: "People with mental illness are dangerous."
- The majority of those who suffer from mental illness do not commit violent crimes. When violence does occur, it usually does so for the same causes as in the wider population, such as feeling intimidated or abusing alcohol and/or drugs excessively.

- Myth: "People with mental illnesses can work low-level jobs, but they're not qualified for really important or responsible jobs."
- Fact: Depending on their individual skills, background, and drive, people with mental disorders

have the capacity to work at any level, just like everyone else.

What is an illustration of how the mind and body interact?

Your thoughts and feelings are interconnected. And how you think may change how you feel. How your body reacts to stress is an illustration of this mind-body link. Regular tension in the muscles, soreness, headaches, and stomach issues may be brought on by constant anxiety and stress about employment, money, or other issues.

Mental diseases

Sometimes referred to as mental health disorders, are a wide category of ailments that affect your emotions, thoughts, and behavior.

A few examples of mental diseases are depression, anxiety disorders, schizophrenia,

- Eating problems,
- And obsessive behaviors.
- Human rights violations,
- Racism,
- And stigma is also frequent.
- Among the most common mental health conditions include anxiety disorders, depression, bipolar disorder, PTSD, and other conditions.
- Neurological disorders.
- Schizophrenia.
- Eating problems.
- Dissociative disorders
- And disruptive behavior.

What triggers issues with mental health?

There are several potential reasons for mental health issues. Although various individuals may be more severely impacted by specific things than others, it is probable that many people are influenced by a complex mix of circumstances.

For instance, the following elements may contribute to a time of poor mental health:

• Social isolation or loneliness, enduring childhood abuse, trauma, or neglect, and being subjected to prejudice and stigma, including racism

• Poverty, socioeconomic adversity, or debt grief (losing a loved one)

- Severe or ongoing stress a physical health issue that has persisted for a long time unemployment or job loss

- Housing issues or homelessness

- Becoming a person's long-term caregiver

- alcohol and drug use Significant trauma as an adult, such as being in battle in the military, being engaged in a major event in which you frightened for your life, or having the victim of violent crime

Why is it crucial to get professional assistance with mental health?

It Takes Courage to Ask for Mental Health Help. Also helpful

It lowers your vulnerability to various health problems.

Other physiological problems might result from poor mental health. Obesity, digestive issues, and other ailments are all connected to insufficient sleep and sleep disturbances. Your chance of acquiring other health issues will be reduced if you get care as soon as possible.

How can you get expert assistance?

Where to Find Licensed Mental Health Professionals - Mental...

If you or someone you love is prepared to seek professional assistance, think about these MHFA curriculum alternatives.

- Please contact your primary care provider.
- Make contact with a mental health specialist.
- Locate a licensed peer expert.
- Call a psychiatrist right now.

How can you tell whether someone needs expert assistance?

- signs that you may want private counseling
- Feeling tense.
- Feeling generally overburdened by it all.

- Over thinking and have difficulty 'switching off' off your thoughts.
- I'm depressed and crying more than normal.
- Getting furious more often or finding it difficult to control your emotions.
- Getting less or more sleep than normal.

The Advantages of Meditation for Mental Health

By focusing on the present moment, encouraging awareness and acceptance, and developing emotional self-control, mindfulness meditation improves mental health.

Keeping my focus on the here and now

Paying attention to the present moment is one of the foundational principles of mindfulness meditation. It includes concentrating on the present moment without passing judgment or allowing anxieties about the past or the future to divert your attention.

By focusing on the here and now, you may improve your mental health and reduce your stress.

You may practice this skill while meditating by paying attention to your breathing. Avoid becoming sidetracked by thoughts of what has to be done later or worrying about something that has already happened by concentrating only on each inhale and exhalation.

Stress and anxiety reduction

It is impossible to emphasize how effective mindfulness meditation is in lowering stress and anxiety because it provides a useful strategy for managing mental health.

By teaching the mind to concentrate on the present moment, mindfulness meditation assists in reducing these unpleasant feelings. With no criticism or ruminating, this technique encourages awareness and acceptance of our ideas and feelings.

For instance, mindfulness meditation enables you to acknowledge overwhelming feelings of fear or insecurity about a fast-approaching project deadline at work while refocusing your attention on things that are under your control, such as your breath or other physical sensations, rather than degenerating into pointless worry.

What are the benefits of self-awareness for mental health?

Understanding Self-Awareness's Importance for Mental Health

Our ability to recognize our emotional triggers and comprehend how we react to them is facilitated by self-awareness. We are more adept at controlling our emotions when we are fearful of them. To control our emotions and prevent overreacting, we may use techniques like deep breathing, meditation, or exercise.

20

Emotional intelligence & mental health: a Relationship

Mental Illness and Emotional Intelligence

Emotional intelligence and mental health issues, particularly anxiety and depression, have been linked in research. More specifically, it was discovered that emotional intelligence is a defense against many illnesses.

Given that emotional intelligence aids in a person's ability to better understand possible stresses, it seems sense that it has an immunizing impact against mental health illnesses. This may lessen emotions of unpleasant hyper arousal and help people with anxiety more quickly return to a calmer state of being by making the environment seem less dangerous.

Being better at recognizing one's feelings may help someone with depression continue to completely absorb difficult situations or losses. As a result, one may be better able to lament the skills, goals, or relationships that have been lost along the way in life and actually be able to move on from the past.

Positive Mental Health and Emotional Intelligence

Comparative to EQ's potential to protect against harmful mental health illnesses, it has been shown that the relationship between mental ability and beneficial, positive mental health is less. However, there has been some evidence linking certain components of emotional intelligence to increased well-being.

Methods for managing stress.
What actions do you take when a deadline is about to pass or your car breaks down? Don't ignore continuous stress symptoms since stress of any kind—chronic, minor, or severe—has a detrimental effect on your body and mind. There will inevitably be difficult moments in life. However, extreme stress, especially if it occurs often, may be harmful to us. Your risk of depression and cardiac problems, such as heart disease, may rise

under conditions of chronic stress like this.

Recognize what your body is experiencing and create simple coping skills to offset the negative consequences of everyday demands.

Stress arises in two different forms:

- Emotional stress may be caused by problems in relationships, pressure at work, money worries, confronting racism, or going through a major life transformation.
- Physical - Physical stress might include being unwell, in

discomfort, having difficulties sleeping, recuperating from an accident, or having a problem with alcohol or drugs.

Fight or flight

Stress, whether it is sudden or ongoing, activates the nervous system and causes the production of the hormones cortical and adrenaline, which raise blood pressure, heart rate, and blood sugar levels. Your body's fight-or-flight reaction is triggered by these changes. This assisted our ancestors in escaping saber-toothed tigers, and it is still helpful today to be safe around risks like car accidents. However, most modern chronic pressures, like financial difficulties or a challenging relationship, keep your body in that elevated condition, which is detrimental to your health.

Effects of High Stress

The majority of us will eventually begin to operate less effectively if we are under constant stress. Given that several studies have connected chronic stress to an increased risk of cardiovascular disease, stroke, depression, weight gain, dementia, and even early death, it's essential to recognize the symptoms of chronic stress.

- Bad sleep for extended periods of time.
- Strong headaches that are frequent.
- Unjustified weight gain or decrease.

- Feelings of worthlessness, disengagement, or isolation.
- Rage and hostility all the time.
- A decline in motivation for activities.
- Constantly fretting or pondering excessively.
- Excessive drug or alcohol consumption.
- Difficulty focusing.

What does the term "positive psychology" mean?

Why Is Positive Psychology Important & What Does It Entail? Positive psychology is a practical approach to achieving peak performance and the scientific study of human wellbeing. It is also known as the study of the qualities and attributes that support the success of people, groups, and organizations. Positive Psychology Institute is the source. What does positive psychology for mental health entail?

Positive Psychology's Relationships with Mental Health

Happiness, hope, motivation, empathy, and self-esteem are all fundamental ideas in positive psychology, and they all directly improve human welfare (Schrank & Slade, 2007). Characterized by joy and the desire to behave in ways that increase pleasure and self-satisfaction.

What are three instances of good mental health?

- Feeling in charge of your life and personal choices is a sign of good mental health.
- Being capable of handling the difficulties and pressures of life.
- Having a healthy mental state, such as the capacity to pay attention at work.
- Having a positive outlook on life in general; feeling physically well.
- Get sufficient rest.

How is mental health connected to happiness?

Overall, the study's results show an inverse association between degrees of happiness and mental health severity. This shows that people were more likely to report lower levels of happiness when they had higher scores on the mental health problem scale.

What does mental health resilience entail?

The capacity to "bounce back from adversity" has been used to characterize resilience, which is a term used to describe both general physical and psychological health. The emphasis of positive psychology has always been on an individual's capacity to enjoy life and strike a balance between their pursuit of psychological goals and their daily activities.

What are the five pillars of resilience in mental health?

Participate in the Five Resilience Pillars during Difficult Times

Self-awareness, mindfulness, self-care, healthy connections, and purpose are the five pillars that make up resilience.

How can you increase your mental toughness?

Although different things will help for various individuals, you might try some of the following:

Take care of yourself. Being nice to oneself may improve how you feel in a variety of circumstances.

Make an effort to relax; pursue your interests and hobbies; spend time in nature.

Take care of your physical well-being.

What does a nurturing connection entail?

Each person in the connection gains from the other's care and attention, which benefits everyone involved. Feeling included and having a feeling of belonging are often characteristics of nurturing relationships. Making others feel desired by them. Supporting other people's wellbeing.

What kind of connection would be considered nurturing?

Techniques for Fostering Relationships

Intentionality is one of the most prevalent types of nurturing conduct of a relationship. You must schedule time just for your companion. You may start by setting up dates, going to the movies, taking a trip, etc. These activities support the growth of closeness in your relationship.

What kind of mental illnesses cause anxiety?
Generalized anxiety disorder, which includes panic disorder with or without apprehension specific phobias, agoraphobia, socially anxious disorder, separation anxiety disorder, and selective mutes are some of the several forms of anxiety disorders.

What are the four forms of mental diseases and the five types of anxiety disorders?

The top five categories of anxiety disorders are as follows:

Obsessive Compulsive Disorder (OCD), Panic Disorder, a condition called post-traumatic stress disorder (PTSD), Social Anxiety Disorder, and Anxiety Disorders Treatment are some of the anxiety disorders that may be treated.

What are the four anxiety coping mechanisms?

1. Examples of coping mechanisms
2. Inhaling deeply.
3. main muscle groups becoming tense and relaxed (progressive muscle relaxation)

4. Either guided imagery or meditation.

What exactly is a mood illness in terms of mental health?

Your emotional state is mostly affected by the mental health issue known as a mood disorder. In patients with mood disorders, extreme emotional highs and lows can endure for protracted periods of time. Although there are many different types of mood disorders, bipolar disorder and depression are two of the more common ones.

What sets depression different from other mood disorders?

Your energy level, cognitive functions (such racing thoughts or lack of attention), sleep, and eating habits may all be affected by symptoms of mood disorders. Feeling depressed most of the time or almost every day is one of the typical symptoms of depression. Lacking vigor or feeling exhausted

How can one recognize depression?

Different individuals are affected by depression in various ways. You can experience numbness or emptiness instead of happiness, sadness, or rage. Depression may sometimes resemble annoyance or exasperation. Little problems seem large all of a sudden.

How can professionals in mental health identify depression?

The mental health professional will make observations of one's attitude and behavior, ask detailed questions about one's reported symptoms (such as how long they last, how intense they are, etc.), how the symptoms affect one's daily life, and may use psychological polls to help determine a diagnosis.

Can Loss and Grief Cause Mental Illness?

Losing a loved one may be traumatizing and very upsetting. You could feel that your daily routine will never be the same while you go through the grief process, which can be perplexing.

Most individuals can eventually come to terms with their loss and resume living their regular lives. Everybody's path to acceptance is unique, and some individuals may need more time than others to get there. Most individuals eventually start to experience the impact of sorrow on mental health; however some people may have considerably more severe symptoms than others.

How is the mental health of adolescents?

There are other symptoms of adolescent mental disorder than depression. A teen's life might be impacted in a number of different ways. Teenagers with poor mental health may struggle in school, with making decisions, and with maintaining their physical health.

Why is the mental health of adolescents important?

Adolescent Mental Health: How Important Is It? | CMC

Youth with poor mental health are more prone to engage in hazardous sexual activity that may lead to unplanned pregnancies, HIV, STDs, and drug abuse, among other health and behavioral risks. The effects of poor mental health last far into adulthood.

What mental traits define adolescence?

Adolescence is a time of mental growth, which includes enhanced capacity for abstract thought.

impulse control.

Creativity.

Decision-making skills and the capacity to solve problems.

How does adult psychological well-being affect things?

It affects our attitudes, feelings, and actions. It also affects how we deal with stress, communicate with others, and make wise choices. Every stage of life—from childhood and youth through adulthood—is crucial for maintaining mental health.

What kind of mental illnesses are common in late adulthood?

Seniors often have mental health problems, which may include, among other things, dementia, psychosis, anxiety and mood disorders, and loneliness. Many older persons have behavioral and sleep problems, cognitive decline, or episodes of confusion as a result of medical diseases or surgical treatments.

How does teenage mental health affect adulthood?

When it comes to their mental health as adults, children and adolescents with mental health problems often show inferior mental health as well as worse levels of life satisfaction overall health-related quality of life.

What connection exists between loneliness and isolation?

No matter how much social interaction there is, loneliness is the sensation of being alone. Lack of social relationships is known as social isolation. Some individuals might get lonely as a result of social isolation, whereas others can become lonely even when they are not socially isolated.

How do you handle isolation and loneliness?
How can I deal with being alone?
Learn how to be at ease in your own company.
Try to be honest with those you know.
Move slowly.
build new relationships.
Avoid comparing yourself to other people.
Take care of yourself.
Check out talking treatments.

www.ingramcontent.com/pod-product-compliance
Lightning Source LLC
Chambersburg PA
CBHW071040260726
48661CB00007B/3076